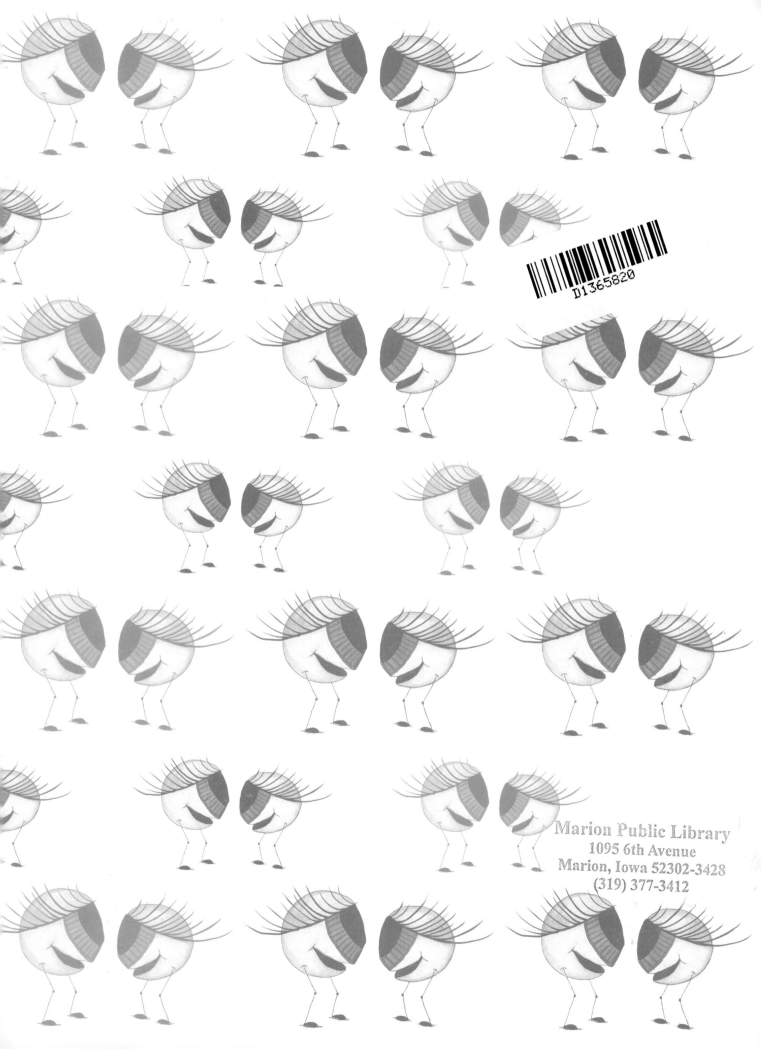

All net profits from this book will be donated

to the Oak Clinic for Multiple Sclerosis.

Vanita Oelschlager

Acknowledgments

Robin Hegan

Jennie Levy

Kristin Blackwood

Sheila Tarr

Cinda Dehner

Eye to Eye
VanitaBooks, LLC
All rights reserved.
© 2014 VanitaBooks, LLC
No part of this book may be reproduced, stored in retrieval systems, or transmitted in any form
or through methods including electronic photocopying, online download, or any other system now known
or hereafter invented – except by reviewers, who may quote brief passages in a review to be printed in a
newspaper or print or online publication – without express written permission from VanitaBooks, LLC.
Text by Vanita Oelschlager.
Illustrations by Robin Hegan.
Design by Jennie Levy.
Printed in China.
ISBN 978-1-938164-06-4 Hardcover
ISBN 978-1-938164-05-7 Paperback

www.VanitaBooks.com

Eye to Eye

a book of **body part idioms**
and **silly pictures**

written by **Vanita Oelschlager**
illustrated by **Robin Hegan**

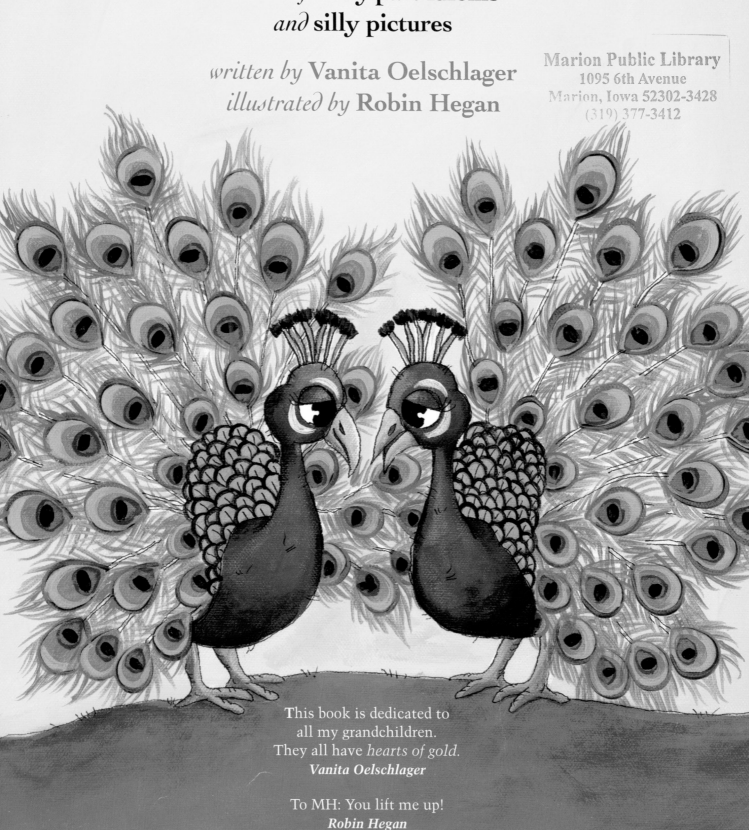

This book is dedicated to
all my grandchildren.
They all have *hearts of gold*.
Vanita Oelschlager

To MH: You lift me up!
Robin Hegan

You are very interested in what another person is saying.

"I want to know what you think. I am *all ears*."

All ears

You keep quiet and don't speak up.

**"She talked so much about her vacation
that we told her to *button her lip*."**

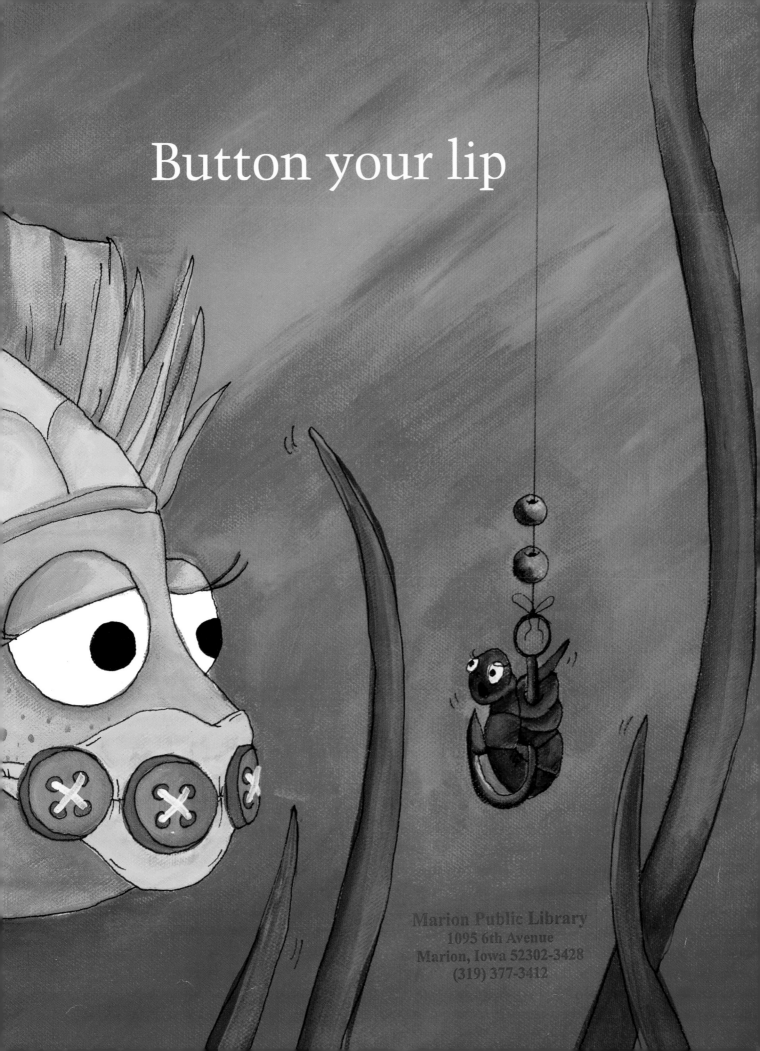

Button your lip

Bone to pick
with you

To have an argument or an unpleasant
matter to settle with someone.

**"Come into my office, I have
a *bone to pick with you*."**

Cold feet

A fear of doing something after you think about it for a while.

"Billy wanted to ask Betty to the dance, but he got *cold feet* when he saw her in class."

Elbow grease

Working hard at a physically difficult job.

"Put a little *elbow grease* into shining that car!"

Cat got your tongue

If you are supposed to say something and you are silent.

"Why don't you answer me? Has the *cat got your tongue?*"

Head over heels in love

You are completely and helplessly in love.

"He fell *head over heels in love* with his kindergarten teacher."

Bury your head
in the sand

To ignore danger by pretending
you don't see it.

**"You are *burying your head in the sand*
if you think that smoking cigarettes
isn't bad for you."**

You like to find things out and are
good at finding the latest news.

**"She always had *a nose for news*, so
no one was surprised when she became
a reporter for the newspaper."**

A nose for news

To take a bold or dangerous risk that people
might not like.

**"If you *stick your neck out* and say what you are
thinking, lots of people may be mad at you."**

Egg on your face

To be embarrassed because of something foolish you did.

"Barb had *egg on her face* when she accidentally broke a lamp at a friend's party."

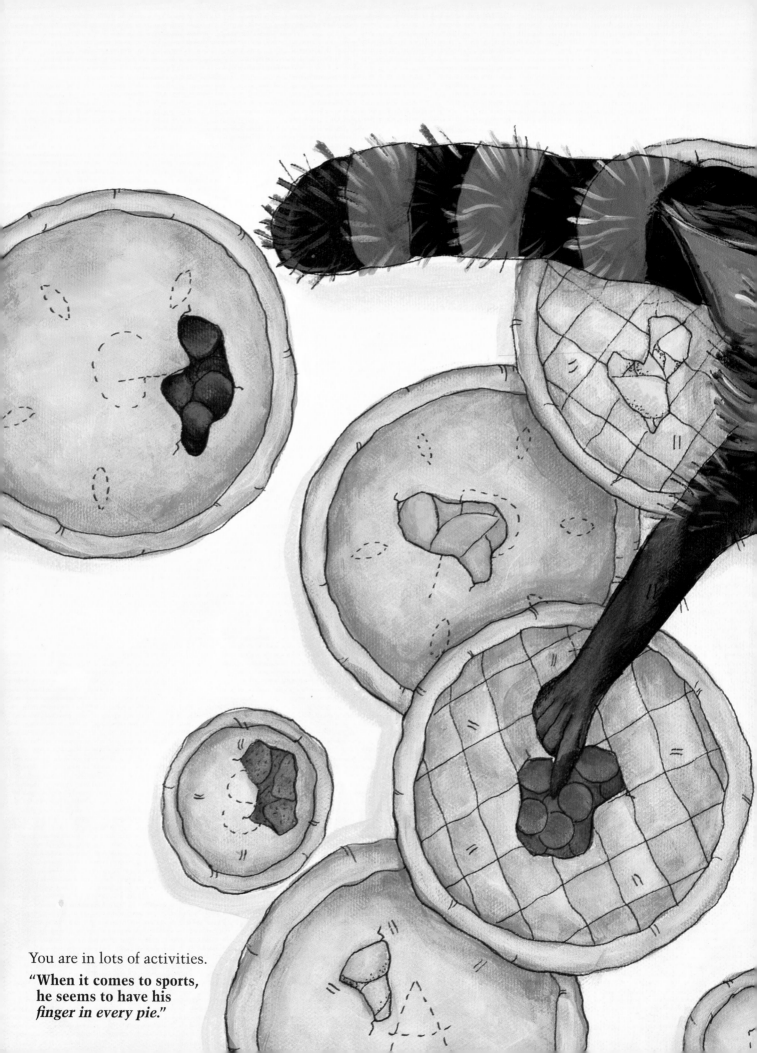

You are in lots of activities.

**"When it comes to sports,
he seems to have his
finger in every pie."**

Finger in every pie

Eyes in the back of your head

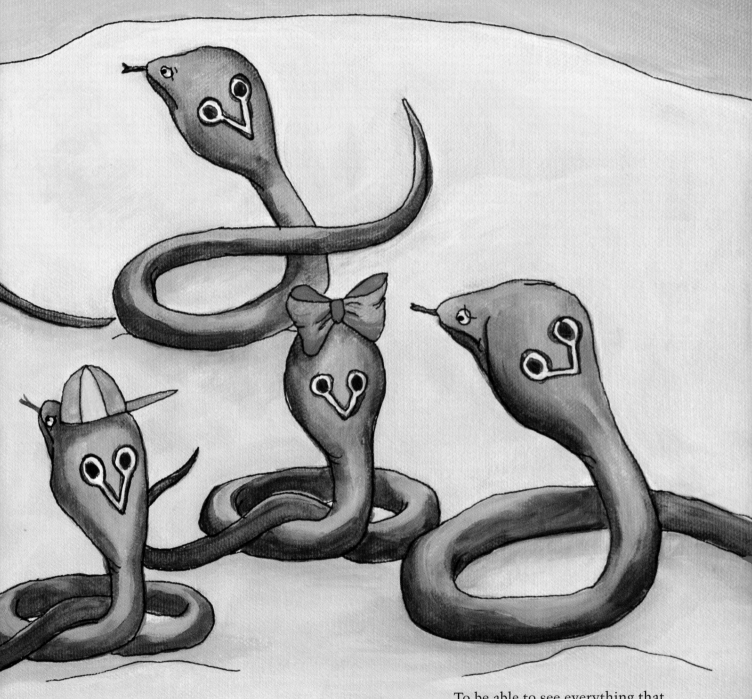

To be able to see everything that is going on around you.

"My teacher always knows when we are passing notes in class. She seems to have *eyes in the back of her head!*"

To hurt someone who tries to help you.

"If you are mean to someone who tries to help, you are *biting the hand that feeds you*."

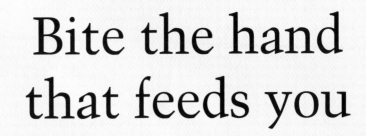

Bite the hand that feeds you

Let your hair down

To relax and let your true self come out.

"At the sleepover, my friends *let their hair down*."

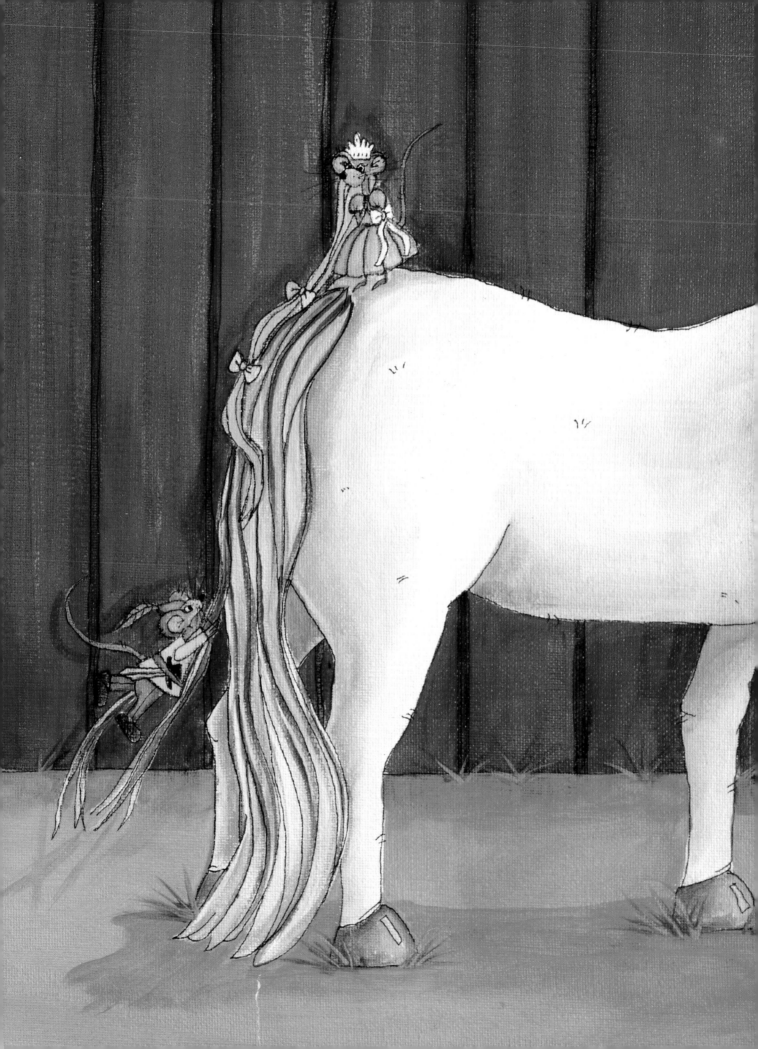

What are idioms?

Every language has "figures of speech", or idioms. They are a short hand way of explaining something unfamiliar or complicated.

The English language has thousands of them. You cannot understand them because the group of words together has little, often nothing, to do with the meanings of the words taken one by one.

Hundreds of years ago, the words might have meant what they said, but today they do not.

In order to understand a language, you must know what the idioms in that language mean. If you try to figure out the meaning of the idiom word by word you're likely to get nowhere – you will get befuddled or confused. You have to know the "hidden" meaning. You need to read between the lines and behind the words.

I am going to show you the "hidden" meaning of some of the idioms in this book. Idioms often show a sense of humor. They're your language's ticklish spots so learning them can be lots of fun. I hope you'll enjoy them as much as we do.

Let your hair down

This idiom started in the 1800s when many women wore their long hair pinned up in public and only let their hair down in private, just before bed.

Egg on your face

This came from rude audiences in the old days throwing raw eggs at the actors they didn't like. To be standing on stage in front of an angry crowd with egg on your face must have been terrible.

Bury your head in the sand

People used to think that because an ostrich had his head in the sand or dirt, he thought if he couldn't see an enemy, the enemy couldn't see him. The ostrich was really looking for seeds and berries and sand to help with digestion. Today "bury your head in the sand" has come to mean refusing to notice a problem or not facing up to reality.

Eye to eye

Vanita Oelschlager is a wife, mother, grandmother, philanthropist, former teacher, current caregiver, author and poet. She is a graduate of the University of Mount Union in Alliance, Ohio, where she currently serves as a Trustee. Vanita is also Writer in Residence for the Literacy Program at The University of Akron. She and her husband Jim received a *Lifetime Achievement Award* from the National Multiple Sclerosis Society in 2006. She won the Congressional *Angels in Adoption*™ *Award* for the State of Ohio in 2007 and was named *National Volunteer of the Year* by the MS society in 2008. She was honored as 2009 *Woman Philanthropist of the Year* by the United Way of Summit County. In May 2011, Vanita received an honorary Doctor of Humane Letters from the University of Mount Union. In 2013, Vanita joined *The LeBron James Family Foundation* to serve on its Advisory Board.

Robin Hegan grew up in the Laurel Mountains of Pennsylvania where imagination took her and her childhood friends on many great adventures. After graduating from The Pennsylvania State University with a degree in Integrative Arts, Robin resided in Ohio for several years until she and her husband, Matt, decided to return to the mountains of Pennsylvania to raise their children. Robin's illustrations can also be seen in *My Grampy Can't Walk, Mother Goose Other Goose, Birds of a Feather, Life is a Bowl Full of Cherries* and *Out of the Blue.* To find out more about Robin, visit www.robinhegan.com.

To agree fully; to have the same opinion.

"The author and illustrator see *eye to eye* when it comes to children's books."

3137

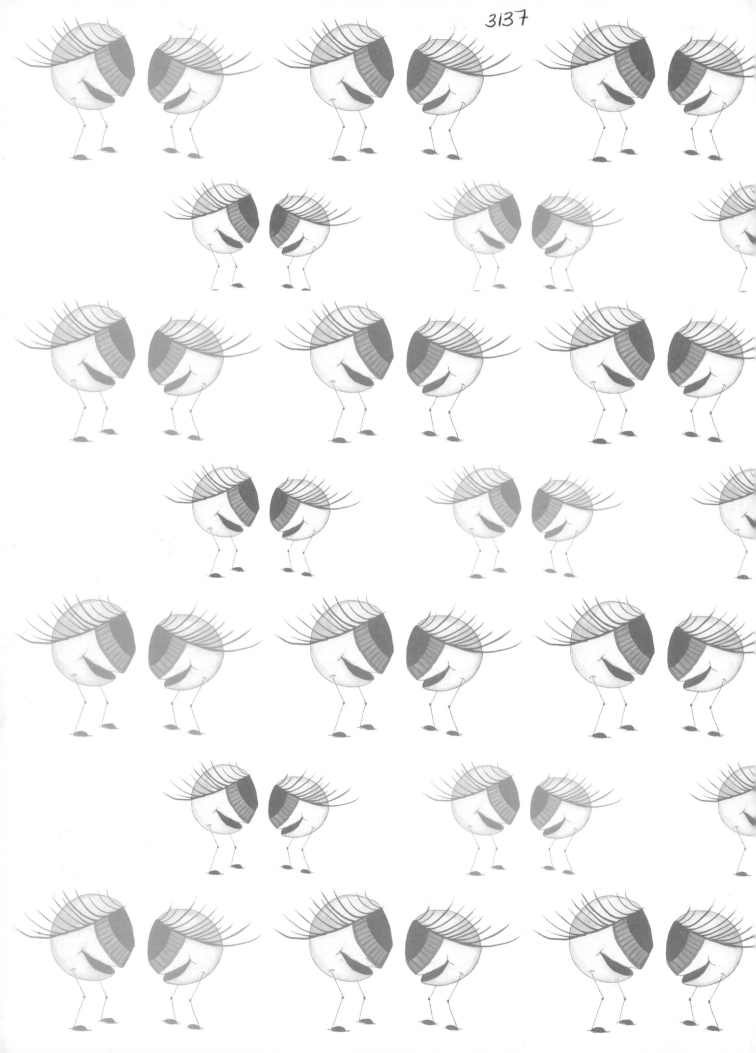